Twenty to M

Knitte
Fast Food

Susie Johns

Search Press

First published in Great Britain 2010

Search Press Limited
Wellwood, North Farm Road,
Tunbridge Wells, Kent TN2 3DR

Reprinted 2011

Text copyright © Susie Johns 2010

Photographs by Debbie Patterson at
Search Press Studios

Photographs and design copyright
© Search Press Ltd 2010

ISBN: 978-1-84448-538-3

Suppliers

If you have difficulty in obtaining any of the
materials and equipment mentioned in this book,
then please visit the Search Press website for
details of suppliers: www.searchpress.com

Printed in Malaysia

Dedication
For my mother and grandmothers
who, by teaching me to knit and
crochet, opened the door to a world
of creative possibilities.

Abbreviations

beg: beginning

dec: decrease (by working two
stitches together)

DK: double knitting

g st: garter stitch (knit every row)

inc: increase (by working into the front and
back of the stitch)

k: knit

k2tog: knit two stitches together

p: purl

psso: pass the slipped stitch over

p2tog: purl two stitches together

rib: ribbing (one stitch knit, one stitch purl)

rem: remain(ing)

rep: repeat(ing)

sl1: slip one stitch on to the left needle
without knitting it

st(s): stitch(es)

st st: stocking stitch (one row knit, one
row purl)

tbl: through back loop

yfwd: yarn forward

Contents

Introduction

In our fast-paced world, snack food is everywhere. From burger joints and hot-dog stands, market stalls and food courts, delicatessens and bakeries, we are offered instant gratification in the form of ready-to-eat pies and pasties, sandwiches and samosas, kebabs, noodles and sweet treats – some familiar, some exotic and some more nutritious than others but all very tasty and tempting.

These knitted versions celebrate the diversity of modern snack foods. They are fun to make and a great way to use up oddments of yarn left over from larger projects.

Some of the patterns are more challenging than others. If you want to start with something simple, try the samosas, fried egg or sushi, then move on to the fish and chips, pasty or ice lolly. More confident or experienced knitters, or those who enjoy the making up of projects and sewing in of yarn ends as well as the knitting, will enjoy making the slices of fruit pie, the pizza, pitta pockets and noodles, while those who like patterns that require you to knit in the round on double-pointed needles – which can be a bit challenging for some – may like to try the hamburger, cupcake, ice cream and biscuits.

These novelty knits would make good gifts; most are designed as 'play food' and are suitable for children as long as you do not add any beads and you sew components together very securely (the pointed wooden skewers should be removed from the kebabs and so should the wooden lollipop sticks).

A note on materials and techniques

Most of the items in this book are made from double knitting yarn. While in some cases suggestions are given for certain yarn compositions – wool, acrylic, and blends containing cashmere, silk, bamboo or alpaca, for example – you should feel free to experiment with the yarns you have available to you. If you need to buy only a small amount of a certain colour, a skein of tapestry yarn may suffice. In a few cases, novelty textured yarns have been used to produce certain effects, such as the 'sprinkles' on a doughnut or the seeds in a slice of wholegrain bread.

Unless otherwise stated, right and wrong sides of work are often interchangeable: just decide which side looks best. Tension (or gauge) are not given: just aim for a firm, close-knit fabric that will hold its shape and not allow the stuffing to poke through, using a larger or smaller needle than the one stated in the pattern, if necessary, to produce the desired effect.

Opposite:
Here is a feast for the eyes! With pasties, pitta pockets, pizza, sandwiches, burgers, prawns, noodles and kebabs, you can knit your own fast food banquet.

Burger

Materials:

3 balls DK yarn – 1 beige, 1 ivory and 1 leaf green

1 ball felting yarn – brown

1 ball silk or rayon yarn – yellow

Polyester fibrefill

Craft foam, 2mm (¹⁄₁₆in) thick

Tapestry needle

Needles:

1 pair 3.00mm (UK 11; US 2) knitting needles

1 pair 3.75mm (UK 9; US 5) knitting needles

Set of four double-pointed 3.00mm (UK 11; US 2) knitting needles

Instructions:

Meat patty (make 1)

With double-pointed 3.00mm (UK 11; US 2) knitting needles and brown felting yarn, cast on 12 sts and divide equally between three needles.

Round 1: k to end.
Round 2: (k1, inc 1 in next st) 6 times [18 sts].
Round 3: k to end.
Round 4: (k2, inc 1 in next st) 6 times [24 sts].
Round 5: k to end.
Round 6: (k3, inc 1 in next st) 6 times [30 sts].
Round 7: k to end.
Round 8: (k4, inc 1 in next st) 6 times [36 sts].
Round 9: k to end.
Round 10: (k5, inc 1 in next st) 6 times [42 sts].
Round 11: k to end.
Round 12: (k6, inc 1 in next st) 6 times [48 sts].
Round 13: k to end.
Round 14: (k7, inc 1 in next st) 6 times [54 sts].
Rounds 15–16: k to end.
Round 17: (k7, k2tog) 6 times [48 sts].
Round 18: k to end.
Round 19: (k6, k2tog) 6 times [42 sts].
Round 20: k to end.
Round 21: (k5, k2tog) 6 times [36 sts].
Round 22: k to end.
Round 23: (k4, k2tog) 6 times [30 sts].
Round 24: k to end.
Round 25: (k3, k2tog) 6 times [24 sts].
Round 26: k to end.
Round 27: (k2, k2tog) 6 times [18 sts].
Round 28: k to end.
Round 29: (k1, k2tog) 6 times [12 sts].

Round 30: k to end.
Round 31: (k2tog) 6 times [6 sts].
Break yarn and thread through rem sts.

Bun (make 2)

With double-pointed 3.00mm (UK 11; US 2) knitting needles and beige double knitting yarn, cast on 12 sts and divide equally between three needles.

Work as for meat patty to Round 15.
Round 16: (k8, inc 1 in next st) 6 times [60 sts].
Round 17: k.
Round 18: (k9, inc 1 in next st) 6 times [66 sts].
Rounds 19-22: k.
Break yarn and join in ivory double knitting yarn.
Rounds 23–24: k.
Round 25: (k9, k2tog) 6 times [60 sts].
Round 26: (k8, k2tog) 6 times [54 sts].
Round 27: (k7, k2tog) 6 times [48 sts].
Round 28: (k6, k2tog) 6 times [42 sts].
Round 29: (k5, k2tog) 6 times [36 sts].
Round 30: (k4, k2tog) 6 times [30 sts].
Round 31: (k3, k2tog) 6 times [24 sts].
Round 32: (k2, k2tog) 6 times [18 sts].
Round 33: (k1, k2tog) 6 times [12 sts].
Round 34: (k2tog) 6 times [6 sts].
Break yarn and thread through rem sts.

Lettuce (make 1)

With size 3.75mm (UK 9; US 5) needles and green double knitting yarn, cast on 14 sts.
Row 1: inc in each st to end [28 sts].
Row 3: (inc 1, k1) to end [42 sts].
Row 4: (inc 1, k2) to end [56 sts].

Row 5: (inc 1, k3) to end [70 sts].
Row 6: (inc 1, k4) to end [84 sts].
Rows 7–13: Starting with a knit row, work st st.
Row 14: k to end.
Cast off; break yarn, leaving long tail.

Mustard (make 1)
With yellow silk or rayon yarn and size 3.00mm (UK 11; US 2) needles, cast on 3 sts.
Row 1: k to end.
Row 2: p to end.
Row 3: inc 1, k1, inc 1 [5 sts].
Rows 4–20: Starting with a purl row, work st st.
Row 21: k2tog, k1, k2tog [3 sts].
Row 23: p to end.
Row 24: k to end.
Cast off; break yarn, leaving long tail.

Making up
For a thin burger, cut one or two circles of craft foam and slip them both inside, then pull up the thread and fasten off to close the holes on the top and base. Pull up the yarn on the last round of the bun and fasten off to close the hole on the 'cut' side of the bun. Stuff the bun with polyester fibrefill through the hole in the top, then neatly stitch the opening closed.

Join the two short edges of the lettuce leaf using the tail of yarn. Join the two side edges of the mustard, then weave in all yarn ends.

You can keep the components separate or stitch them together, sandwiching the meat patty with the lettuce between two buns. The finished bun measures 8.5cm (3⅜in) across.

Can I Have a Cheeseburger, Please?
Surely the most ubiquitous of all fast food, take your pick from a hamburger with mustard or a tasty cheeseburger. To add a sprinkling of sesame seeds to the top of the bun, thread a tapestry needle with ivory yarn and make a series of small single stitches in a random pattern. To make the cheese, use size 3.75mm (UK 9; US 5) needles and yellow cotton yarn. Cast on 18 sts and work 30 rows in g st (knit every row), then cast off.

Cheese Sandwich

Materials:

2 balls acrylic or wool DK flecked yarn –
  1 light beige and 1 beige

1 ball bamboo blend DK yarn – yellow

Craft foam, 2mm (1/16in) thick

Polyester fibrefill

Tapestry needle and thread

Needles:

1 pair 3.00mm (UK 11; US 2)
  knitting needles

1 pair 4.00mm (UK 8; US 6)
  knitting needles

Instructions:

Bread (make 4)
With size 3.00mm (UK 11; US 2) needles, cast
on 20 sts in light beige yarn.
Rows 1–34: k to end.
Rows 35–36: inc 1, k to last st, inc 1 [24 sts].
Rows 37–40: g st.
Row 41: dec 1, k to last 2 sts, k tog [22 sts].
Row 42: k to end.
Rows 43 and 44: as row 41 [18 sts].
Cast off.

Crust (make 2)
With size 3.00mm (UK 11; US 2) needles, cast
on 4 sts in beige yarn.
Row 1: sl1, k3.
Rep row 1 until work measures 38cm (15in) or is
the right length to fit around the edges of the
bread slice.
Cast off.

Cheese (make 1)
With size 4.00mm (UK 8; US 6) needles, cast on
16sts in yellow yarn.
Row 1: sl1, k to end.
Rows 2–33: Rep row 1.
Cast off.

Making up
Using the finished bread as a template, cut two
pieces of craft foam. To make up one slice of
bread, arrange a thin layer of polyester fibrefill
on the wrong side of one bread piece, top
it with craft foam, add a few more wisps of
polyester fibrefill, then top with a second piece
of bread.

Pin and stitch a crust all round and oversew
the edges of the crust to each bread piece.
Repeat for a second slice of bread. Place the
cheese in between the two slices of bread and
secure with a few stitches, if you wish.

The finished sandwich measures
approximately 12cm (4¾in) long, 11cm (4½in)
wide and 5cm (2in) thick.

Lunch Break

Fast food does not have to be junk food.
A heathy wholegrain sandwich is quick to
prepare even when it is this knitted version.
For a white bread sandwich, knit the bread
slices in white or off-white. To make a slice of
ham, follow the instructions for the cheese but
use yarn in a suitable shade of pink.

Pizza Slice

Materials:

5 balls DK yarn – 1 beige, 1 red, 1 dark red, 1
   green, 1 off-white

1 ball cotton DK yarn – white

1 ball 4-ply silk yarn – yellow

1 ball 4-ply cotton yarn – coral

Tapestry needle

Needles:

1 pair 3.75mm (UK 9; US 5) knitting needles

1 pair 3.00mm (UK 11; US 2) knitting needles

1 pair of 4.50mm (UK 7; US 7) knitting needles

Two double-pointed 3.75mm (UK 9; US 5)
   knitting needles

Instructions:

Base (make 1)
With size 3.75mm (UK 9; US 5) needles and
beige yarn, cast on 1 st.
Row 1: k into front, back and front of st [3 sts].
*Row 2: sl1, k to end.
Rows 3–4: Rep row 2.
Row 5: inc 1, k to last st, inc 1.**
Rep from * to ** until there are 31 sts.
Next row: cast off 3 sts, k to end [28 sts].
Next row: cast off 3 sts, k to end [25 sts].
Next row: cast off 4 sts, k to end [21 sts].
Next row: cast off 4 sts, k to end [17 sts].
Next row: cast off 5 sts, k to end [12 sts].
Next row: cast off 5 sts, k to end [7 sts].
Cast off rem 7 sts.

Crust (make 1)
With two 3.75mm (UK 9; US 5) double-pointed
needles and beige yarn, cast on 3 sts.
Row 1: k3; do not turn but slide sts to other end
of needle.
Rep row 1 until cord is long enough to fit
around outer edge of crust.

Tomato sauce (make 1)
With size 4.50mm (UK 7; US 7) needles and red
yarn, cast on 1 st.
Row 1: k into front, back and front of st [3 sts].
Continue as for base, rep instructions from * to
** until there are 19 sts.
Next row: k2tog, k3, inc 1, k3, sl1, k2tog, psso,
k3, inc 1, k1, k2tog [17 sts].
Next row: k2tog, k2, inc 1, k2, sl1, k2tog, psso,
k2, inc 1, k2, k2tog [15 sts].
Next row: k7, turn and cast off; break yarn.
Rejoin yarn to rem 8 sts, k to end, then cast off.

Cheese (make 2)
With size 4.50mm (UK 7; US 7) needles and
yellow yarn, cast on 9 sts.
Rows 1–11: g st (knit every row).

Pepperoni (make 6)
With size 3.00mm (UK11; US 2) needles and
coral yarn, cast on 3sts.
Row 1: inc in each st to end [6 sts].
Row 2: k to end.
Row 3: inc in each st to end [12 sts].
Row 4: inc in each st to end [24 sts].
Cast off.
Stitch row ends together, to form a disc. Thread
tapestry needle with length of dark red yarn
and work blanket stitch around perimeter, stitch
by stitch, on cast-off row..

Pepper slice (make 3)
With size 3.00mm (UK11; US 2) needles and
green yarn, cast on 12 sts.
Row 1: k2tog tbl 6 times.
Cast off.

Mushroom (make 4)

With size 3.75mm (UK 9; US 5) needles and white yarn, cast on 4 sts.
Rows 1–4: g st (knit every row).
Row 5: k1, (inc 1) twice, k1 [6 sts].
Row 6: inc in each st to end [8 sts].
Cast off.

Making up

Stitch the crust to the curved edge of the base.
Stitch the tomato sauce on to the base.

If desired, thread the tapestry needle with green yarn and work a scattering of small stitches all over the tomato sauce, like flecks of herbs.

Next, choose your toppings. To stitch the pepperoni in place, use off-white yarn and small stitches to represent flecks of fat. For all of the other toppings, use matching yarns to stitch them in place, trying to make the stitches as discreet as possible.

Just Like Mamma Used To Make

Create your own favourite topping combinations. Here one slice is topped with pepperoni while the other combines mushrooms, cheese and green peppers. The finished pizza slice, with topping, measures approximately 15cm (6in) long, 14cm (5½in) wide and 1cm (⅜in) thick.

11

Bacon and Egg

Materials:

2 balls wool or cashmere blend DK yarn –
   1 ivory and 1 yellow

1 ball 4-ply cotton yarn – brick red

Polyester fibrefill

Tapestry needle and thread

1 button, 3cm (1⅛in) diameter

Instructions:

Bacon (make 2)

Begin by making the rind. With 3.00mm (UK 10;
US 3) double-pointed needles and ivory, cast
on 3 sts.

Row 1: k3; do not turn but slide sts to other end
of needle.

Rows 2–62: Rep row 1; then cast off, but do not
break yarn.

Row 63: Using same yarn and needles, pick up
and k 41 sts (including st already on needle
after casting off), evenly spaced, along the
length of the cord; do not break yarn.

Rows 64–65: Join in brick red yarn and work in g
st; do not break yarn.

Row 66: (RS) With ivory yarn, k to end; do not
break yarn but slide the sts to the other end of
the needle.

Row 67: (RS) With brick red yarn, k to end.

Row 68: (WS) With ivory yarn, p to end; do not
break yarn but slide the sts to the other end of
the needle.

Row 69: (WS) With brick red yarn, p to end.

Row 70: (RS): With ivory yarn, k to end;
break yarn and slide sts to the other end
of the needle.

Rows 71–73: (RS) With brick red yarn, and
starting with a p row, work st st.

Cast off.

Egg white (make 1)

With 3.25mm (UK 10; US 3) needles and ivory or
white yarn, cast on 8 sts.

Row 1: k to end.

Row 2: p to end.

Rows 3–10: Cont in st st, inc 1 st at each end of
next 6 rows and then 1 st at each end of next 2
alt rows [24 sts].

Needles:

1 pair 3.25mm (UK 10; US 3) knitting needles

Two double-pointed 3.00mm (UK 11;
US 2) knitting needles

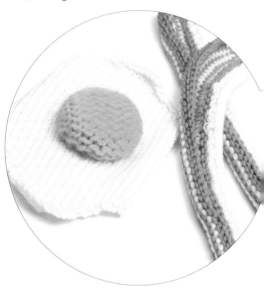

Rows 11–24: Work 14 rows in st st without
further shaping.

Row 25: (RS) k2tog, k to last 2 sts, k2tog.

Row 26: p to end.

Rows 27–28: Rep last two rows once more.
[20 sts].

Rows 29–34: Cont in st st, dec 1 st at each end
of next 6 rows [8 sts].

Row 35: k to end.

Row 36: p to end.

Cast off.

Egg yolk (make 1)

With size 3.25mm (UK 10; US 3) needles and
yellow yarn, cast on 6 sts.

Row 1: k to end.

Row 2: inc 1, k to end.

Rows 3–11: Rep row 2 [16 sts].

Rows 12–23: g st.

Row 24: k2tog, k to end [15 sts].

Rows 25–33: Rep row 24 [6 sts].

Cast off, leaving a tail of yarn.

Making up
Thread a tapestry needle with the tail of yarn from the egg yolk and run a gathering stitch all round the edge. Place the button inside, with a few wisps of polyester fibrefill for extra padding, then pull up the yarn end tightly to gather up and enclose the button. Secure it with a few stitches, then stitch it to the egg white. The finished bacon rashers are approximately 18cm (7in) long and 3.5cm (1⅜in) wide, while the egg measures approximately 12cm (4¾in) in diameter.

Full English Breakfast
Here we have the great British breakfast, delicious and satisfying. It takes no time at all, with yarn and needles, to create a couple of crisp rashers and a perfect fried egg – free range, of course! Why not make a sausage (see instructions on page 15) to add to the egg and bacon, and turn your breakfast into a real slap-up meal?

Hot Dog

Materials:

3 balls wool DK yarn – 1 brown, 1 beige and 1 ivory

1 ball 4-ply silk or rayon yarn – yellow

Polyester fibrefill

Tapestry needle

Needles:

1 pair 3.00mm (UK 11; US 2) knitting needles

Set of four 3.00mm (UK 11; US 2) double-
pointed knitting needles

Instructions:

Frankfurter (make 1)

With the set of four size 3.00mm (UK 11;
US 2) needles and brown double knitting
yarn, cast on 18 sts and divide equally
between three needles.
Knit 60 rounds.
Break yarn and thread through each stitch.

Bread roll:

Crust (make 2)

With size 3.00mm (UK 11; US 2) needles,
cast on 6 sts in beige yarn.
Row 1: inc1, k1, (inc 1) twice, k1, inc1 [10 sts].
Row 2: inc, k3, (inc 1) twice, k3, inc1 [14 sts].
Row 3: k6, (inc 1) twice, k6 [16 sts].
Row 4: k.
Row 5: k7, (inc 1) twice, k7 [18 sts].
Rows 6–61: g st.
Row 62: k7, (k2tog) twice, k7 [16 sts].
Row 63: k.
Row 64: k6, (k2tog) twice, k6 [14 sts].
Row 65: k2tog, k3, (k2tog) twice, k3,
k2tog [10 sts].
Row 66: k2tog, k1, (k2tog) twice, k1,
k2tog [6 sts].
Row 67: k to end.
Cast off.

Bread (make 2)

With 3.00mm (UK 11; US 2) needles, cast on
5 sts in ivory yarn.
Row 1: k1, (inc 1, k1) twice [7 sts].
Row 2 and each even-numbered row: k.
Row 3: k1, inc 1, k3, inc 1, k1 [9 sts].

Row 5: k1, inc 1, k5, inc 1, k1 [11 sts].
Row 7: k1, inc 1, k7, inc 1, k1 [13 sts].
Rows 8–54: g st.
Row 55: k1, k2tog, k7, k2tog, k1 [11 sts].
Row 57: k1, k2tog, k5, k2tog, k1 [9 sts].
Row 59: k1, k2tog, k3, k2tog, k1 [7 sts].
Row 61: k1, (k2tog, k1) twice [5 sts].
Cast off.

Mustard (make 1)

With two 3.00mm (UK 11; US 2) double-pointed
needles, cast on 3 sts in yellow yarn.
Row 1: k3; do not turn but slide sts to other end
of needle.
Rep this row until work measures 20cm (7¾in);
fasten off.

Making up

Pull up the yarn on the last round of the sausage
and fasten it off to close the hole. Stuff the
sausage through the cast-on edge, then neatly
stitch the opening closed.

Thread matching yarn through each end of
the bread roll crust and pull up very slightly to
gather, then stitch the bread to the crust, leaving
a small opening; stuff and stitch opening closed.
Stitch the bread rolls together along one long
edge, leaving the other edge open. Stitch the
mustard to the frankfurter, bending it into a
wiggly line as you go. You can either stitch the
frankfurter in place or, if it is intended as part of a
play food set, leave the two items separate.

The finished frankfurter measures 16cm (6¼in)
in length; the bread roll measures 15cm (6in).

Sausages

Plump and inviting, who could resist this delicious frankfurter nestling within a soft bread roll with a tantalising wiggle of mustard?
For a hearty British breakfast, knit a sausage to accompany the egg and bacon on page 14. Follow the method for the frankfurter but use brown double knitting yarn, cast on only 12 stitches and work only 50 rounds.

Pitta Pocket

Materials:

5 balls wool DK yarn – 1 beige, 1 light beige,
   1 leaf green, 1 white and 1 pink

Polyester fibrefill

Tapestry needle

Needles:

1 pair 3.00mm (UK 11; US 2) knitting needles

Instructions:

Pitta bread (make 1)

With size 3.00mm (UK 11; US 2) needles, cast on
7 sts in beige yarn.
*Row 1: k.
Row 2: cast on 2, k to end.
Rows 3–5: Rep row 2 [15 sts].
Row 6: inc 1, k to end.
Rows 7–15: Rep row 6 [25 sts]*.
Rows 16–55: g st.
**Row 56: k2tog, k to end.
Rows 57–65: Rep row 56 [15 sts].
Row 66: cast off 2, k to end.
Rows 67–69: Rep row 66 [7 sts]**.
Rep from Row 1 once more.
Cast off.

Chicken (make 5)

With size 3.00mm (UK 11; US 2) needles, cast on
11 sts in light beige yarn.
Row 1: k5, p1, k5.
Row 2: p5, k1, p5.
Row 3: k5, p1, k5.
Row 4: p5, k1, p5.
Row 5: k2tog, k3, p1, k3, k2tog [9 sts].
Row 6: p4, k1, p4.
Row 7: k4, p1, k4.
Row 8: p4, k1, p4.
Row 9: k2tog, k2, p1, k2, k2tog [7 sts].
Row 10: p3, k1, p3.
Row 11: k3, p1, k3.
Row 12: p3, k1, p3.
Row 13: k2tog, k1, p1, k1, k2tog [5 sts].
Row 14: p2, k1, p2.
Row 15: k2, p1, k2.
Row 16: p2, k1, p2.
Cast off.

Lettuce strip (make 9)

With size 3.00mm (UK 11; US 2) needles, cast on
15 sts in leaf green yarn.
Row 1: (inc 1, k1) 7 times, inc 1 [23 sts].
Cast off.

Onion ring (make 3 pink and 2 white)

With size 3.00mm (UK 11; US 2) needles and
pink yarn, cast on 38 sts using the cable
method; break yarn.
With white yarn, k2tog tbl 19 times. Cast off.
For white onion, use white yarn throughout.

Making up

Fold the pitta bread in half along the 'hinge',
with right sides together, and stitch the edges
together with backstitch, leaving one long
edge open. Fold 3mm (⅛in) to the inside along
the opening and slip stitch to form a neat
hem before turning right sides out. Fold each
chicken piece in half with the purl side outwards
and oversew the sides together (adding a tiny
amount of stuffing, if you wish). Join the ends of
each onion ring strip to form a ring.

Knitting notes

When sewing up the chicken pieces, there is
no need to be too neat, as uneven stitches will
help to create a more lopsided, authentic look.
To stuff the chicken pieces, instead of polyester
stuffing, use short lengths of yarn salvaged
after weaving in ends, as they will create a more
lumpy appearance.

   The finished pitta pocket measures
approximately 17cm (6¾in) long and 11cm
(4¼in) wide.

Half Pitta

A Middle Eastern flat bread is cut open and filled with crisp lettuce and slivers of chicken – but you can vary the filling according to your taste. Make as many pieces of chicken, lettuce strips and onion rings as you wish. For the not-so-hungry, half a pitta bread will suffice. Using the same yarn and needles, cast on 25 sts and work 25 rows, then follow the pattern from ** to ** then from * to * and work a further 25 rows without shaping before casting off. Stitch side seams and turn under a 3mm (⅛in) hem on the open edge, as before.

Sushi

Maki

Uramaki

Nigiri

Materials:

4 balls wool DK yarn – 1 red or orange, 1 green,
  1 yellow and 1 coral

1 ball 4-ply silk or rayon yarn – ivory

Polyester fibrefill

Black rayon or satin ribbon, 24mm (1in) wide

Sewing needle and black thread

Tapestry needle

Needles:

1 pair 3.00mm (UK 11; US 2) knitting needles

Instructions:

Maki (made in one piece)

With size 3.00mm (UK 11; US 2) needles and red
or orange DK yarn, cast on 5 sts.
Row 1–8: Starting with a k row, work st st.
Rows 9–20: Break yarn and join in green yarn.
Work a further 12 rows in st st.
Row 21: Change to ivory yarn, used double.
(k1, p1) to end of row.
Rows 22–65: Rep row 21.
Cast off, leaving a tail of yarn for stitching.

Uramaki filling

With size 3.00mm (UK 11; US 2) needles and
yellow yarn, cast on 5 sts.
Rows 1–12: k. Cast off.

Uramaki rice

With size 3.00mm (UK 11; US 2) needles and
ivory yarn, used double, cast on 6 sts.
Row 1: (k1, p1) to end of row.
Rows 2–72: Rep row 1.
Cast off, leaving a tail of yarn for stitching.

Nigiri rice

With size 3.00mm (UK 11; US 2) needles and
ivory yarn, cast on 3 sts.
*Row 1: p1, k1, p1.
Row 2: as row 1.
Row 3: inc 1, k1, inc 1 [5 sts].
Row 4: k1, (p1, k1) twice.
Rows 5–22: Rep row 4.
Row 23: k2tog, k1, k2tog [3 sts].**
Rep from * to ** twice more.

Next row: p1, k1, p1.
Cast off, leaving a tail of yarn for stitching.

Nigiri topping

With size 3.00mm (UK 11; US 2) needles and
yellow or coral yarn, cast on 3 sts.
Row 1: p3.
Row 2: inc 1, k1, inc 1 [5 sts].
Rows 3–21: Starting with a p row, work st st.
Row 22: k2tog, k1, k2tog [3 sts]. Cast off.

Making up

For maki, roll up the strip, starting with the cast-
on edge, and stitch the cast-off edge to the roll,
using the tail of yarn to stop it from unrolling.
Then cut a piece of ribbon long enough to go
round the outside of the roll with an extra 4mm
(⅛in) for overlap. With black thread, stitch one
end of the ribbon to the roll, wrap around, fold
under the remaining end and stitch it neatly in
place over the first end.

For uramaki, roll up the filling and secure it
with one or two stitches. Cut a piece of ribbon
long enough to encase the filling with an extra
4mm (⅛in) for overlap, wrap around, fold under
the remaining end and stitch neatly in place
using black thread. Secure one end of the rice
strip to the ribbon, then continue rolling. Once
finished, stitch the cast-off edge to the roll,
using the tail of yarn.

For nigiri, fold the rice in three, forming
a three-layered piece, and stitch the sides
together, adding a few wisps of stuffing

18

between layers, if necessary. Secure the topping in place with a few stitches. Cut a 10cm (4in) length of ribbon, fold in the edges to form a narrow strip, then wrap it around the roll and stitch the ends together underneath.

Sushi

As good to look at as it is to eat, a plate of sushi is a visual delight. Here, silky yarn represents rice while ribbon 'seaweed' encases each delicious morsel. Maki (the ribbon-covered round pieces) and uramaki (the white round pieces) are 3cm (1⅛in) in diameter; while nigiri (the long ribbon-wrapped pieces) are each 7cm (2¾in) long.

Cornish Pasty

Materials:

2 balls DK yarn – 1 beige and 1 leaf green

Polyester fibrefill

Tapestry needle

Needles:

1 pair 3.00mm (UK 11; US 2) knitting needles

Two double-pointed 3.00mm (UK 11; US 2) knitting needles

Instructions:

Pastry (make 1)

With size 3.00mm (UK 11; US 2) needles and beige yarn, cast on 14 sts.
Row 1 (RS): p to end.
Row 2: inc 1, k to last st, inc 1 [16 sts].
Rows 3–16: Rep rows 1 and 2 [30 sts].
Rows 17–23: Starting with a p row, work st st without further shaping.
Row 24: k2tog, k to last 2 sts, k2tog [28 sts].
Row 25: p to end.
Rows 26–39: Rep last 2 rows [14 sts].
Cast off.

Crimp (make 1)

With size 3.00mm (UK 11; US 2) double-pointed needles and beige yarn, cast on 4 sts.
Row 1: k4; do not turn but slide sts to other end of needle.
Rep this row until work measures 30cm (12in); fasten off, leaving tail of yarn for sewing.

Parsley stem (make 1)

With size 3.00mm (UK 11; US 2) double-pointed needles and green yarn, cast on 2 sts.
Row 1: k2; do not turn but slide sts to other end of needle.
Rep this row until work measures 3cm (1⅛in) in length.

Parsley leaves

*Next row: inc 2 in each st [4 sts].
Next row: inc 2 in each st [8 sts].**
Cast off but do not break yarn.
There is one st on needle; pick up 1 st from end of cord, at base of leaves you have just made, and rep from * to ** once more.
Cast off, leaving a tail of yarn.

Making up

Fold the pastry in half, with the RS (purl side) outwards and stitch the edges together using the tapestry needle and spare yarn, leaving a small gap. Insert stuffing through the gap, then close it with a few more stitches. Thread the tail of yarn at the end of the cord on to the tapestry needle and gather the cord by passing the needle right through, from side to side in a zigzag motion, on every fourth row, then pull up until the crimped cord fits around the seam of the pasty. Stitch it in place.

Use the tail of yarn to secure the ends of the parsley leaves to top of stalk, encouraging the leaves to form clusters as you do so.

The finished pasty measures approximately 13cm (5in) long, 5cm (2in) wide and 3cm (1⅛in) deep.

Pasty and Empanada

A savoury filling encased in a circle of pastry, folded and crimped, was the snack of choice for Cornish miners – and you will find variations on this theme all round the world.

To make an empanada, a Spanish and South American version, use a paler coloured yarn and make up with the knit side outwards. Make a cord just long enough to fit along the seam, without gathering, and stitch it in place.

Meat Pie

Materials:
1 ball DK yarn – beige
Polyester fibrefill
Tapestry needle
Craft foam, 1cm (⅜in) thick

Needles:
1 pair 3.00mm (UK 11; US 2) knitting needles
Set of four double-pointed 3.00mm (UK 11; US 2) knitting needles

Instructions:

Pie (make 1)
With size 3.00mm (UK 11, US 2) double-pointed needles and beige yarn, cast on 6 sts and divide between three needles; use fourth needle to knit.
Round 1: k.
Round 2: inc in each st [12 sts].
Round 3: (k1, inc 1) 6 times [18 sts].
Round 4: (k2, inc 1) 6 times [24 sts].
Round 5: (k3, inc 1) 6 times [30 sts].
Continue in this way, knitting 1 extra st between each increase, until there are 108 sts.
Next round: p to end.
Next round: (k1, p1) to end.
Rep last round twice more.
Next round: *k1, (p1, k1) 7 times, sl1, k2tog, psso, rep from * 5 times more [96 sts].
Next round: (k1, p1) to end.
Rep last round twice more.
Next round: *k1, (p1, k1) 6 times, sl1, k2tog, psso, rep from * 5 times more [84 sts].
Next round: (k1, p1) to end.
Next round: p.
Next round: (k5, k2tog) 12 times [72 sts].
Next round: (k10, k2tog) 6 times [66 sts].
Next round: (k9, k2tog) 6 times [60 sts].
Next round: (k8, k2tog) 6 times [54 sts].
Continue in this way, knitting 1 fewer st between each decrease, until there are 36 sts, then insert a circle of craft foam, approximately 9cm (3¾in) in diameter, through the hole in the centre, to create a flat base.
Next round: (k4, k2tog) 6 times [30 sts].
Next round: (k3, k2tog) 6 times [24 sts].
Next round: (k2, k2tog) 6 times [18 sts].

Next round: (k1, k2tog) 6 times [12 sts].
Next round: (k2tog) 6 times [6 sts].
Cut yarn, leaving a tail, and thread through rem sts.

Crimped edge
Using size 3.00mm (UK 11, US 2) double-pointed needles, and distributing stitches between three needles, pick up and k 108 sts on purl ridge around top edge of pie.
Round 1: inc in each st [216 sts] and cast off.

Pastry leaves (make 3)
With size 3.00mm (UK 11, US 2) needles and beige yarn, cast on 1 st.
Row 1 (WS): inc 2 (k into front, back and front of st) [3 sts].
Row 2: k1, p1, k1.
Row 3: k1, inc 2 (as in row 1), k1 [5 sts].
Row 4: k1, (p1, k1) twice.
Row 5: k1, inc 1, p1, inc 1, k1 [7 sts].
Row 6: k1, (p2, k1) twice.
Row 7: k3, p1, k3.
Rows 8–11: Rep rows 6 and 7.
Row 12: Rep row 6.
Row 13: k1, k2tog, p1, k2tog, k1 [5 sts].
Row 14: k1, (p1, k1) twice.
Row 15: k1, sl1, k2tog, psso, k1 [3 sts].
Row 16: p3tog.
Fasten off.

Making up
Insert stuffing through the small hole in the centre of the pie, then pull up the tail of the yarn and fasten off. Stitch the pastry leaves to the top of the pie. The finished pie measures approximately 12cm (4¾in) in diameter.

Hearty Lunch

Creating a pie, with crisp pastry enclosing a delicious sweet or savoury filling, is a labour of love – but if someone else makes it, it is definitely fast food!

23

Prawn

Materials:

1 ball DK yarn – pink

Polyester fibrefill

Tapestry needle

Sewing needle and pink thread

Two small black beads for eyes

Needles:

1 pair 3.00mm (UK 11; US 2) knitting needles

Two 3.00mm (UK 11; US 2) double-pointed
    knitting needles

Instructions:

Head (make 1)

With size 3.00mm (UK 11; US 2) needles and
pink yarn, cast on 4 sts.

Row 1: k each st tbl.

Row 2: k to end.

Row 3: p to end.

Row 4: inc 1, p2, inc 1 [6 sts].

Row 5: k to end.

Row 6: inc 1, p to last st, inc 1.

Rep rows 5 and 6 twice more [12 sts].

Cast off.

Body (make 1)

With size 3.00mm (UK 11; US 2) needles and
pink yarn, cast on 10 sts.

Row 1: k to end.

Row 2: p to end.

Rows 3–4: g st.

Rows 5–12: rep rows 1–4 twice.

Rows 13: k2tog, k6, k2tog [8 sts].

Rows 14–17: Rep rows 1–4 once.

Row 18: p2tog, p4, p2tog [6 sts].

Rows 19–21: k to end.

Row 22: (p2tog) 3 times [3 sts].

Row 23: k to end.

Row 24: p to end.

Row 25: inc in each st [6 sts].

Row 26: inc in each st [12 sts].

Row 27: (k1, p1) to end.

Rep row 27 three times.

Cast off in rib and fasten off, leaving a tail of
yarn for sewing.

Antennae (make 1)

With size 3.00mm (UK 11; US 2) double-pointed
needles and pink yarn, cast on 2 sts.

Row 1: k2; do not turn but slide sts to other end
of needle.

Rep this row until work measures 10cm (4in);
fasten off.

Making up

Join the head to the body with the tapestry
needle and spare yarn. Run the tail of the
yarn down each edge of the body and pull
up slightly, to create a curved shape. Stitch
the edges of the body (not including the tail)
together and stuff lightly, then stuff the head
and close the seam. For legs, knot several
strands of yarn to the underside, at the base of
the head.

   Stitch two beads in place for eyes, one on
each side of the head, using a sewing needle
and pink thread, then fold the antennae piece
in half and stitch it to the head.

Prawn Again
Prawns are a tasty seafood snack – fresh, light and healthy!

Fish 'n' Chips

Materials:

1 ball DK yarn – beige
1 ball wool/silk blend sock yarn – pale yellow
Polyester fibrefill
Craft foam, 1cm (⅜in) thick
Tapestry needle

Needles:

1 pair 2.25mm (UK 13; US 1) knitting needles
1 pair 2.75mm (UK 12; US 2) knitting needles

Instructions:

Fish in batter (make 2)

With size 2.75mm (UK 12; US 2) needles and
beige yarn, cast on 5 sts.
Row 1: k1, (p1, k1) twice.
Row 2: as row 1.
Row 3: inc 1, p1, k1, p1, inc 1 [7 sts].
Row 4: p1, (k1, p1) three times.
Row 5: inc 1, k1, (p1, k1) twice, inc 1.
Row 6: k1, (p1, k1) to end.
Row 7: inc 1, p1, (k1, p1) three times, inc 1.
Row 8: p1, (k1, p1) to end.
Rows 9–12: rep rows 5–8 once more [15 sts].
Rows 13–14: p1, (k1, p1) to end.
Row 15: inc 1, k1, (p1, k1) six times, inc 1 [17 sts].
Row 16: k1, (p1, k1) to end.
Rows 17–26: rep row 16 11 times more.
Row 27: k1, k2tog, p1, (k1, p1) to last 3 sts,
k2tog, k1 [15 sts].
Row 28: p1, (k1, p1) to end.
Rows 29–30: rep row 28.
Row 31: p1, p2tog, k1, (p1, k1) to last 3 sts,
p2tog, p1 [13 sts].
Row 32: k1, (p1, k1) to end.
Rows 33–34: rep row 32.
Row 35: k1, k2tog, p1, (k1, p1) to last 3 sts,
k2tog, k1 [11 sts].
Row 36: p1, (k1, p1) to end.
Row 37: p1, p2tog, k1, (p1, k1) to last 3 sts,
p2tog, p1 [9 sts].
Row 38: k1, (p1, k1) to end.
Row 39: k1, k2tog, p1, k1, p1, k2tog, k1 [7 sts].
Rows 40–41: p1, (k1, p1) to end.

Row 42: inc 1, k1, (p1, k1) twice, inc 1 [9sts].
Row 43: k1, (p1, k1) to end.
Row 44: inc 1, p1, (k1, p1) three times, inc 1.
Row 45: p1, (k1, p1) to end.
Rows: 46–51: Rep row 45 six times more.
Cast off.

Chips (make at least 5)

With size 2.25mm (UK 13; US 1) needles and
yellow yarn, cast on 17 sts.
Row 1: p to end.
Row 2 (RS): k to end.
Row 3: p to end.
Rows 4–5: as row 3.
Rows 6–14: rep rows 2–5 twice more.
Row 15: cast on 3 sts, k to end [20 sts].
Row 16: Cast on 3 sts, p to end [23 sts].
Cast off purlwise.

Chunky chips (make at least 5)

With size 2.25mm (UK 13; US 1) needles and
yellow yarn, cast on 21 sts.
Row 1 (RS): k to end.
Row 2: p to end.
Row 3: k to end.
Row 4: p to end.
Rows 5–6: k to end.
Rows 7–18: rep rows 1–6 twice more.
Row 19: cast on 4 sts, k to end [25 sts].
Row 20: cast on 4 sts, p to end [29 sts].
Row 21: k to end.
Rows 22–23: p to end.
Cast off.

Making up

Stitch the two batter pieces together around the edges; leave a small gap and insert polyester fibrefill, then stitch the gap closed. Cut the foam into strips the same length as the chips. Place the foam on the WS of the work, adding a few wisps of polyester fibrefill for extra padding if necessary. Wrap the knitted fabric round and join the side and end seams using spare yarn. The finished fish measures approximately 14cm (5½in) long and 7cm (2¾in) wide, and the chips are approximately 7cm (2¾in) long. The chunky chips are a little larger at 8cm (3in) long.

Salt and Vinegar?

This classic British takeaway treat of fish in crisp batter, accompanied by golden chips, is irresistible. Garnish it with a sprig of parsley, following the instructions on page 20.

Noodles

Materials:

5 balls DK yarn – 1 beige, 1 white, 1 russet, 1
  red and 1 green
1 ball 4-ply silk or rayon yarn – pale yellow
Tapestry needle

Needles:

1 pair 3.25mm (UK 10; US 3) knitting needles
Two double-pointed 3.00mm (UK 11; US 2)
knitting needles

Instructions:

Noodles (make at least 20)
With size 3.00mm (UK 11; US 2) double-pointed
needles and pale yellow yarn, cast on 3 sts.
Row 1: k3; do not turn but slide sts to other end
of needle
Rep this row until cord measures approximately
30cm (12in) long.

Crispy pork slices (make at least 3)
With size 3.25mm needles and beige yarn, cast
on 10 sts.
Break yarn and join in white.
Row 1: k each st tbl.
Row 2: sl1, k to end.
Row 3: rep row 2.
Break yarn and join in russet.
Row 4: k1, (k2tog, k)] three times [7 sts].
Row 5: sl1, k to end.
Rows 6–14: rep row 5.
Cast off.

Spring onions and peppers (make 3 of each)
Using the same needles and exactly the same
method as for the noodles, but knitting fewer
rows, make short lengths of cord in green and
white and red yarn to represent small pieces of
the different vegetable.

Making up
Weave in all of the loose ends, then arrange the
noodles in a cardboard Chinese food carton
and scatter the other items on top.

Pork Chow Mein!

Eaten straight from the takeaway carton, noodles are a satisfying snack, especially with a few tasty slices of crispy pork alongside delicious shreds of spring onion and red pepper.

Shish Kebab

Materials:

3 balls wool or acrylic DK yarn – 1 brown, 1 green and 1 red

1 ball of cotton DK yarn – beige

Craft foam, or washing-up sponge 2.5cm (1in) thick

Polyester fibrefill

Wooden or bamboo skewers

Tapestry needle

Instructions:

Meat cube (make 3)
With size 3.25mm (UK 10; US 3) needles and brown DK yarn, cast on 6 sts.
Rows 1–9: p.
Rows 10–18: k.
Rows 19–27: p.
Row 28: cast on 7 sts, k6, p1, k6 [13 sts].
Row 29: cast on 7 sts, k6, p1, k6, p1, k6 [20 sts].
Rep last row 8 times more. Cast off.

Pepper chunk (make 3 in red and 2 in green)
With 3.25mm (UK 10; US 3) needles and red or green DK yarn, cast on 21 sts.
Row 1: k10 tbl, p1, k10 tbl.
Row 2: k10, p1, k10.
Rows 3–4: rep row 2.
Row 5: k1, (k2tog, k1) 3 times, p1, (k1, k2tog) 3 times, k1 [15 sts].
Row 6: k7, p1, k7.
Rows 7–9: rep row 6.
Row 10: k1, (k2tog, k1) twice, p1, (k1, k2tog) twice, k1 [11 sts].
Row 11: k5, p1, k5.
Rows 12–14: rep row 11.
Cast off, leaving a tail of yarn for sewing up.

Mushroom (make 3)
With four 3.00mm (UK 11; US 2) double-pointed needles and beige DK yarn, cast on 6 sts and divide between three needles.
Round 1: k to end.
Round 2: inc in each st [12 sts].
Round 3: k to end.
Round 4: (k1, inc 1) 6 times [18 sts].
Round 5: k to end.
Round 6: (k2, inc 1) 6 times [24 sts].

Needles:

1 pair 3.25mm (UK 10; US 3) knitting needles

Set of four double-pointed 3.00mm (UK 11; US 2) knitting needles

Round 7: k to end.
Round 8: (k3, inc 1) 6 times [30 sts].
Rounds 9 and 10: k to end.
Round 11: (k3, k2tog tbl) 6 times [24 sts].
Round 12: (k2, k2tog tbl) 6 times [18 sts].
Round 13: (k1, k2tog tbl) 6 times [12 sts].
Round 14: (k2tog) 6 times [6 sts].
Rounds 15–20: k.
Break yarn and thread through rem sts.

Making up
Cut a cube of craft foam or washing-up sponge to fit inside the cube of meat. Place it on the wrong side of the work and draw up the knitted fabric to enclose it. Stitch the seams by oversewing edges with the tapestry needle and spare yarn. For the pepper, fold the work in half and oversew the edges. Stuff the mushroom firmly and tie off the end of the stalk. Push a wooden or bamboo skewer through the knitted pieces, in any order you like. The meat cubes are approximately 3.5cm (1¼in) and the mushrooms are 4cm (1½in) in diameter.

Any Sauce With That?

Comprising chunks of meat, skewered and grilled, sometimes with vegetables, the shish kebab is one of the tastiest treats to come from the Middle East and is easy to replicate using yarn and needles. Make a vegetarian version, if you like, with mushrooms replacing the meat.

31

Cherry Pie

Materials:

1 ball DK yarn – beige
1 ball aran weight wool yarn – deep pink
Craft foam, 2.5cm (1in) thick
Polyester fibrefill
Tapestry needle

Needles:

1 pair 3.25mm (UK 10; US 3) knitting needles
1 pair 3.75mm (UK 9; US 5) knitting needles

Instructions:

Pastry (made in 1 piece):

With size 3.25mm (UK 10; US 3) needles and
beige yarn, cast on 24 sts.
Row 1: p to end.
Row 2: k to end.
Row 3: p to end.
Row 4: k1, (yfwd, k2tog) to last st, k1.
Row 5: p to end.
Row 6: k to end.
Row 7: To form crimped edge of pastry,
fold work and k each st together with
corresponding st from cast-on row.

Outer edge

Starting with a k row, continue in stocking stitch
for 10 rows.
Purl 2 rows.

Base

Next row: k1, sl1, k1, psso, k to last 3 sts,
k2tog, k1.
Next row: p to end.
Next row: k to end.
Next row: p to end.
Rep last 4 rows until 6 sts rem.
Next row: k1, sl1, k1, psso, k2tog, k1.
Next row: p to end.
Next row: k to end.
Next row: p to end.
Next row: (k2tog) twice.
Next row: p2tog.
Fasten off.

Top crust

With WS facing, pick up and k 24 sts along
lower edge of hem on crimped edge. Work as
for base.

Cherry filling (make 1)

With size 3.75mm (UK 9; US 5) needles, cast on
47 sts.
Row 1: k2, then k1, yfwd, k1, yfwd, k1 into
same stitch; turn and p5; turn and k5; turn, sl2
knitwise, k3tog, psso. Repeat another fourteen
times, k2.
Row 2: p to end.
Row 3: k4, then k1, yfwd, k1, yfwd, k1 into
same stitch; turn and p5; turn and k5; turn, sl2
knitwise, k3tog, psso. Repeat 14 times, k1.
Row 4: p to end.
Cast off.

Making up

Cut a wedge of foam to fill the pastry. Pad
out with a few wisps of polyester fibrefill all
round. Stitch the edges of the filling to the top
and base of pastry. The finished slice of pie
measures 15cm (6in) long, 10cm (4in) wide and
4cm (1½in) deep.

Sweet Ol' Blueberry Pie

A slice of pie is a wonderful indulgence… especially when it has a juicy, fruity filling as shown here. For the blueberry filling, which does not involve knitting bobbles, use a purple bouclé yarn. With 3.25mm (UK 10; US 3) needles, cast on 8 sts and work in garter stitch (knit every row) to make a strip 25cm (10in) long.

Iced Doughnut

Materials:

1 ball acrylic blend DK yarn – white with coloured flecks

1 ball acrylic or wool yarn – light beige

Polyester fibrefill

Tapestry needle

Needles:

Set of four 3.00mm (UK 11; US 2) double-pointed knitting needles

Instructions:

Doughnut

With size 3.00mm (UK 11; US 2) double-pointed needles and white yarn with coloured flecks, cast on 60 sts and divide between three needles.
Rounds 1–5: k to end.
Round 6: (k4, k2tog) 10 times [50 sts].
Rounds 7–8: knit 2 rounds.
Round 9: (k3, k2tog) 10 times [40 sts].
Rounds 10–11: knit 2 rounds.
Round 12: (k2, k2tog) 10 times [30 sts].
Rounds 13–14: knit 2 rounds.
Round 15: (k1, k2tog) 10 times [20 sts].
Rounds 16–17: knit 2 rounds. Break yarn; join in light beige.
Rounds 18–19: knit 2 rounds.
Round 20: (k1, inc 1) 10 times [30 sts].
Rounds 21–22: knit 2 rounds.
Round 23: (k2, inc 1) 10 times [40 sts].
Rounds 24–25: knit 2 rounds.
Round 26: (k3, inc 1) 10 times [50 sts].
Rounds 27–28: knit 2 rounds.
Round 29: (k4, inc 1) 10 times [60 sts].
Rounds 30–31: knit 2 rounds.
Cast off, leaving a tail of yarn for sewing up.

Making up

Thread the tapestry needle with the tail of yarn and, with the right side facing outwards, stitch the cast-on and cast-off edges together, leaving a small gap. Stuff the doughnut with polyester fibrefill until it is firm, then sew the gap closed. The finished doughnut measures approximately 10cm (4in) in diameter and is 3.5cm (1⅜in) thick.

Raspberry Doughnut

Definitely not a health food! Doughnuts are a very popular sweet snack, and come in a myriad of flavours. Instead of a speckled yarn, use a soft angora or mohair blend in deep raspberry pink and use a sewing needle and thread to stitch on clear glass seed beads in a random pattern to represent a light dusting of sugar crystals.

Ice Cream

Materials:

1 ball cotton 4-ply yarn – straw yellow

1 ball soft bouclé yarn – white

1 ball acrylic DK yarn – chocolate brown

Craft foam, 2mm (1/16in) thick

Polyester fibrefill

Tapestry needle

Needles:

Set of four 2.75mm (UK 12; US 2) double-pointed knitting needles

1 pair 4.00mm (UK 8; US 6) knitting needles

Instructions:

Cone (make 2)

With set of four 2.75mm (UK 12; US 2) needles and straw yellow yarn, cast on 6 sts and divide between three needles.

Round 1: (k1, p1) 3 times.

Round 2: as round 1.

Round 3: k to end.

Rounds 4–5: as round 1.

Round 6: inc in each st to end [12 sts].

Rounds 7–8: (k1, p1) 6 times.

Round 9: k to end.

Rounds 10–11: (k1, p1) 6 times.

Round 12: (inc 1, k2, inc 1) 3 times [18 sts].

Rounds 13–14: (k1, p1) 9 times.

Round 15: k to end.

Rounds 16–17: (k1, p1) 9 times.

Round 18: (inc 1, k4, inc 1) 3 times [24 sts].

Rounds 19–20: (k1, p1) 12 times.

Round 21: k to end.

Rounds 22–23: (k1, p1) 12 times.

Round 24: (inc 1, k3) 6 times [30 sts].

Rounds 25–26: (k1, p1) 15 times.

Round 27: k to end.

Rounds 28–29: (k1, p1) 15 times.

Round 30: (inc 1, k4) 6 times [36 sts].

Rounds 31–32: (k1, p1) 18 times.

Round 33: k to end.

Rounds 34–35: (k1, p1) 18 times.

Round 36: (inc 1, k5) 6 times [42 sts].

Rounds 37–38: (k1, p1) 21 times.

Round 39: k to end.

Rounds 40–41: (k1, p1) 21 times.

Round 42: (inc 1, k6) 6 times [48 sts].

Rounds 43–44: (k1, p1) 24 times.

Round 45: k to end.

Rounds 46–47: (k1, p1) 24 times.

Round 48: (p1, k1) to end.

Round 49: (k1, p1) to end.

Rounds 50–53: rep rounds 48 and 49 twice. Cast off.

Soft scoop (make 1)

With size 4.00mm (UK 8; US 6) needles and white yarn, cast on 24 sts.

Rows 1–2: st st. Begin with a k row.

Row 3: (k3, inc 1) to end [30 sts].

Rows 4–6: st st. Begin with a p row.

Row 7: (k4, inc 1) to end [36 sts].

Rows 8–10: st st. Begin with a p row.

Row 11: (k5, inc 1) to end [42 sts].

Rows 12–14: st st. Begin with a p row.

Row 15: (k6, inc 1) to end [48 sts].

Row 16: p to end.

Row 17: (k6, k2tog) to end [42 sts].

Row 18: p to end.

Row 19: (k5, k2tog) to end [36 sts].

Rows 20–24: st st. Begin with a p row.

Row 25: (k4, k2tog) to end [30 sts].

Row 26: p to end.

Row 27: (k3, k2tog) to end [24 sts].

Row 28: p to end.

Row 29: (k2, k2tog) to end [18 sts].

Row 30: p to end.
Row 31: (k1, k2tog) to end [12 sts].
Row 32: p to end.
Row 33: (k2tog) 6 times [6 sts].
Rows 34–38: st st. Begin with a p row.
Row 39: (k2tog) 3 times [3 sts].
Row 40: p3.
Row 41: sl1, k2tog, psso; fasten off, leaving a tail of yarn for sewing.

Chocolate flake (make 1)

With 4.00mm (UK 8; US 6) needles and brown DK yarn, cast on 20 sts.
Row 1: (k1, p1) to end.
Rep row 1 until work measures 10cm (4in). Cast off ribwise.

Making up

Cut a semicircle of craft foam, roll it into a cone and place it inside the knitted cone, making sure that the edges are below the cast-off edge. Stuff the cone with polyester fibrefill. Roll up the flake and secure it by stitching with the tapestry needle and spare yarn. Create small pleats in the fabric of the soft scoop and secure it with a few firm stitches, then stitch up the seam, leaving a gap about halfway down. Insert the chocolate flake into the gap, then stuff firmly. Stitch the soft scoop to the cone on the inside of the rim. The finished ice cream measures approximately 22cm (8¾in) tall.

Round scoop for the strawberry ice cream (make 1)

With set of four 2.75mm (UK 12; US 2) needles and pink yarn, cast on 24 sts and divide between three needles.
Round 1: k to end.
Round 2: p to end.

Strawberry Dream

A scoop of delicious ice cream in a crisp, biscuity cone is a great reminder of sunshine and days out. Making the round scoop with pink yarn will produce a mouth-watering strawberry cornet.

Round 3: (k3, inc 1) 6 times [30 sts].
Rounds 4–5: k.
Round 6: (k4, inc 1) 6 times [36 sts].
Rounds 7–8: k.
Round 9: (k5, inc 1) 6 times [42 sts].
Rounds 10–11: k.
Round 12: (k6, inc 1) 6 times [48 sts].
Rounds 13–16: k to end.
Round 17: (k6, k2tog) 6 times [42 sts].
Round 18: k to end.
Round 19: (k5, k2tog) 6 times [36 sts].
Cont in this way, working 1 fewer st between decreases on every other round, until 12 sts rem.
Next round: (k2tog) 6 times [6 sts].
Break yarn and thread through rem sts. Pull up and fasten off.

Ice Lolly

Materials:

4 skeins tapestry yarn – 1 bright pink, 1 yellow,
   1 green and 1 light brown

Craft foam, 2mm (¹⁄₁₆in) thick

Polyester fibrefill

Tapestry needle and thread

Flat wooden lolly stick

Needles:

2 pairs 3.00mm (UK 11; US 2) knitting needles

Instructions:

Lolly (make 2)

*With size 3.00mm (UK 11; US 2) needles and
pink yarn, cast on 7 sts.

Row 1: k each st tbl.

Row 2: p to end.**

Break yarn and transfer work to a spare needle.
Rep from * to **.

Row 3: k to end, cast on 2 sts, k across sts on
spare needle [16 sts].

Row 4: p to end.

Rows 5–16: st st. Begin with a k row. Break yarn;
join in yellow.

Rows 17–28: st st. Begin with a k row. Break
yarn; join in green.

Rows 29–34: st st. Begin with a k row.

Row 35: k1, sl1, k1, psso, k to last 3 sts,
k2tog, k1 [14 sts].

Row 36: p to end.

Rows 37–40: Rep rows 35 and 36 twice more
[6 sts].

Cast off.

Stick (make 1)

*With size 3.00mm (UK 11; US 2) needles and
light brown yarn, cast on 7 sts.

Beg with a k row, work 20 rows in st st. Break
yarn, leaving a 25cm (10in) tail; thread
through all sts.

Making up

Pull up the tail of the yarn at the base of the stick,
then stitch the sides together. Insert the lolly stick.
Cut a piece of foam to fit inside the lolly; pad
out on both sides with polyester fibrefill. Stitch
the side seams of the lolly using the tapestry
needle and spare yarn to match. Insert the end
of the stick into the base of the lolly and stitch
the cast-on edges together, securing the lolly to
the stick with a few neat stitches. The finished
lolly measures approximately 19cm (7½in) long
(including stick) and 6cm (2⅜in) wide.

Yarn note

You could use any DK weight yarn for this project;
as so little of each colour is needed, small skeins
of tapestry wool, available in a dazzling choice of
colours, are an ideal choice.

Popsicle

Straight from the freezer, what could be more refreshing on a hot day? For a woolly version of this frozen delight, use the most colourful yarns in your basket. Use your own combination of colours, such as three different shades of orange, to suggest juicy fruit flavours. If the lolly is designed as play food for a child, do not use a wooden stick.

Cupcake

Materials:

4 balls DK yarn – 1 white, 1 beige, 1 pink
  and 1 red

Craft foam, 2mm (¹⁄₁₆in) thick

Polyester fibrefill

Tapestry needle

Needles:

Set of four 3.00mm (UK 11; US 2) double-
  pointed knitting needles

1 pair 3.75mm (UK 9; US 5) knitting needles

1 pair 3.00mm (UK 11; US 2) knitting needles

Instructions:

Cake case (make 1)

With the set of four size 3.00mm (UK 11; US 2)
double-pointed needles and white yarn,
cast on 6 sts and distribute them between
three needles.

Round 1: k to end.
Round 2: inc in each st [12 sts].
Round 3: (k1, inc 1) 6 times [18 sts].
Round 4: (k2, inc 1) 6 times [24 sts].
Round 5: (k3, inc 1) 6 times [30 sts].
Round 6: (k4, inc 1) 6 times [36 sts].
Round 7: (k5, inc 1) 6 times [42 sts].
Round 8: (k1, p1) to end.
Rounds 9–19: Rep round 8.
Round 20: (yfwd, k2tog) to end.
Rounds 21–25: Rep round 8.
Cast off, leaving a tail of yarn for sewing.

Cake (make 1)

With 3.00mm (UK 11; US 2) needles and beige
yarn, cast on 6 sts.
Work in g st until work measures 18cm (7in).
Cast off.

Icing (make 1)

With 3.75mm (UK 9; US 5) needles and pink
yarn, cast on 9 sts.
Row 1: k to end.
Row 2: p to end.
Rep rows 1 and 2 until work measures 40cm
(15¾in). Cast off.

Cherry (make 1)

With 3.00mm (UK 11; US 2) needles and red
yarn, cast on 3 sts.
Row 1: inc 1, k to last st, inc 1.
Row 2: p to end.
Rows 3–6: Rep rows 1 and 2 twice [9 sts].
Row 7: k to end.
Row 8: p to end.

Row 9: k2tog, k to last 2 sts, k2tog.
Rows 10–13: Rep rows 8 and 9 twice [3 sts].
Cast off, leaving a tail of yarn.

Making up

Fold the last five rows of the cake case to the
inside and slip stitch into place. To make the
cake, join the ends of the beige piece to make
a ring; insert this into the case and slip stitch it
in place. At this stage, if you wish, cut a circle
of craft foam to place in the bottom of the cake
case, to create a stable, flat base. Fold the icing
in half lengthways and stitch the sides together
using the tapestry needle and thread. Roll up
the folded icing into a spiral, securing it with a
few stitches, then insert it into the centre of the
case. To make the cherry, thread the tapestry
needle with the tail of yarn and run the needle
in and out of stitches all round the edge of
the knitted piece. Place a ball of stuffing in the
centre and pull up tightly, enclosing the filling,
to create a ball shape. Stitch it to the top of the
cake. The finished cake is approximately 5cm
(2in) high and 7.5cm (3in) in diameter.

Lemon Fancy

*This dainty teatime treat could easily be
gobbled up in a couple of mouthfuls.
A luxury yarn has been used to make the icing
on these cakes but you could use any double-
knitting weight yarn you like. If the cake is to
be used as a decoration (and not as play food
for children) you could decorate the top with
a little flower, using 40cm (15¾in) of narrow
purple ribbon for the petals and 9cm (3½in) of
wire-edged green ribbon to make leaves.*

Samosa

Materials:

1 ball cotton DK yarn – yellow ochre
Polyester fibrefill
Tapestry needle and thread

Needles:

1 pair 3.25mm (UK10; US 3) knitting needles

Instructions:

Samosa

With size 3.25mm (UK10; US 3) needles and
yellow ochre yarn, cast on 49 sts.
Row 1: sl1, k to end.
Row 2: k1, k2tog, k to last 3 sts, k2tog, k1.
Row 3: sl1, k to end.
Row 4: rep row 3.
Rep rows 2–4 until 5 sts remain.
Next row: k1, sl1, k2tog, psso, k1 [3 sts].
Next row: k to end.
Next row: sl1, k2tog, psso; fasten off.

Making up

Fold, bringing the point at the top of the
triangle (where the work was fastened off) to
the centre of the cast-on row, then fold in the
two sides, forming a triangle of four layers.
Stitch the edges together, adding a little
stuffing for a plump result.

Fusion Food

*The samosa is a crispy Indian snack comprising a spicy filling encased in
a tempting triangle of pastry, and it is a firm favourite the world over.
Spring rolls and samosas are from different culinary traditions but these
knitted versions pair up very nicely. The finished samosa, knitted in a
cotton yarn, with an exotic saffron hue, measures approximately 10cm
(4in) long. To make the spring roll, use a wool DK yarn in medium-
brown and, instead of folding the knitted fabric into a triangle, roll it up,
tucking in the sides as you go, then secure with a few stitches.*

Biscuit

Materials:

1 ball DK yarn – biscuit beige
1 ball soft bouclé yarn – white
Craft foam, 2mm (¹⁄₁₆in) thick
Tapestry needle

Needles:

1 set of four 3.00mm (UK 11; US 2) double-
  pointed knitting needles
1 set of four 4.00mm (UK 8; US 6) double-
  pointed knitting needles

Instructions:

Basic biscuit (make 2)

With set of four size 3.00mm (UK 11; US 2)
needles and biscuit beige yarn, cast on 6 sts
and divide equally between three needles.
Round 1: k to end.
Round 2: inc in each st to end [12 sts].
Round 3: (k1, inc 1) 6 times [18 sts].
Round 4: (k2, inc 1) 6 times [24 sts].
Round 5: (k3, inc 1) 6 times [30 sts].
Round 6: (k4, inc 1) 6 times [36 sts].
Round 7: (k5, inc 1) 6 times [42 sts].
Round 8: (k6, inc 1) 6 times [48 sts].
Round 9: (k7, inc 1) 6 times [54 sts].
Round 10: (k8, inc 1) 6 times [60 sts].
Round 11: k to end.
Round 12: (k8, k2tog) 6 times [54 sts].
Round 13: (k7, k2tog) 6 times [48 sts].
Round 14: (k6, k2tog) 6 times [42 sts].
Do not cast off but break yarn, leaving a long
tail. Thread this through rem sts.

Creamy filling (make 1)

With set of four size 4.00mm (UK 8; US 6)
needles and white yarn, cast on 6 sts and divide
equally between three needles.
Rounds 1–8: Follow the instructions for the
basic biscuit.
Round 9: k to end.
Round 10: (k6, k2tog) 6 times [42 sts].
Round 11: (k5, k2tog) 6 times [36 sts].
Do not cast off but break yarn, leaving a long
tail. Thread this through rem sts.

Making up

Cut a circle of foam 6cm (2¼in) in diameter and
place it on the wrong side of the knitted biscuit.
Pull up the yarn until the knitting fits snugly,
then fasten it off. Do the same with the creamy
filling but use a 5.5cm (2⅛in) circle of foam.

To make a custard cream, sandwich the filling
between two biscuits.

Knitting notes

The finished biscuit measures approximately
6.5cm (2½in) in diameter and 1.5–2cm
(½–¾in) thick.

Milk and Cookies

*Most people like a biscuit to accompany a cup of
tea or coffee and fill the gap between meals, and
they make a lovely pre-bedtime treat. Here are
knitted versions of a couple of old favourites.
To make a chocolate biscuit, use chocolate brown
double-knitting yarn and follow the instructions
for the basic biscuit, omitting rounds 10 and 12.
Stitch this topping to a single basic biscuit, with
right sides up.*

Acknowledgments:

For many of the projects requiring double knitting (or sports weight) yarn, such as the cup cakes, prawns, egg and sandwiches, I used Sublime Cashmere Merino Silk DK; for projects requiring a yarn with a silky finish, such as the noodles, the sushi rice and the mustard on the hot dog, I used 4-ply silk yarn from Knitshop.co.uk; and for the chips, I used Regia Silk sock yarn. Thank you to everyone who has supplied me with yarns. Thanks also to members of Knitting Night at The Pelton for their encouragement and feedback.

You are invited to visit the author's website:
www.susieatthecircus.typepad.com

Susie is also a member of the Ravelry online knitting community:
www.ravelry.com

Publishers' Note

If you would like more books about novelty knitting, try:
Knitted Flowers by Susie Johns, Search Press 2009;
Knitted Cakes by Susan Penny, Search Press 2008;
and *Knitted Bears* by Val Pierce, Search Press 2009; all from the *Twenty to Make* series.